In Heavenly Love Abiding

In Heavenly Love Abiding

Robert Chapman

Guardian BOOKS

Belleville, Ontario, Canada

ISBN: 1-55306-309-0

For more information or
to order additional copies, please contact:
Lt.-Col. Robert Chapman
108 305 34th Street
Prince Albert, SK S6V 8B8
(306) 754-6520 Fax: (306) 763-8436

Guardian Books is an imprint of *Essence Publishing,* a Christian Book Publisher dedicated to furthering the work of Christ through the written word.
For more information, contact:
44 Moira Street West, Belleville, Ontario, Canada K8P 1S3.
Phone: 1-800-238-6376 Fax: (613) 962-3055
E-mail: info@essencegroup.com
Internet: www.essencegroup.com
Printed in Canada
by

Table of Contents

In Heavenly Love Abiding

In heavenly love abiding,
    No change my heart shall fear;
And safe is such confiding,
    For nothing changes here.
The storm may roar without me,
    My heart may low be laid;
But God is round about me,
    And can I be dismayed?

Wherever He may guide me,
    No want shall turn me back;
My Shepherd is beside me,
    And nothing can I lack.
His wisdom ever waketh,

His sight is never dim;
He knows the way He taketh,
And I will walk with Him.

Green pastures are before me,
Which yet I have not seen;
Bright skies will soon be o'er me,
Where the dark clouds have been.
My hope I cannot measure,
My path to life is free;
My Saviour has my treasure,
And He will walk with me.

—*Anna Laetitia Waring (1823-1910)*

*This song was sung at the funeral service of
Ross and Timothy Chapman,*

*and at the memorial service for
Bob and Ruth Chapman.*

Acknowledgements

I am not unmindful of the encouragement and help of others in my mission to write this book. I am indebted to the many who have made contributions in tributes and remembrances: to my wife of fifty years, Alvina, for the design and inspiration for the front cover; to Lieutenant.-Colonel Max Ryan for reading the manuscript and offering helpful counsel; to Pete Kluck for writing the Foreword, and to the Holy Spirit who gave guidance in all aspects of this undertaking.

Foreword

Bob and Ruth Chapman made a difference, not just because of who they were, but because of *Whose* they were. Abandoned to God's call, they allowed the Lord to use them and refine them, even through deep and painful waters, until the day they were promoted to Glory.

Daily, through six years of working side by side with Bob to lead the work of Bible translation in Cameroon, I saw Bob and his wife, Ruth, trust God and seek His wisdom. They modeled Christ-like character and compassion. Their strong testimony to the grace of God working in the lives of two faithful disciples of Jesus Christ leaves a wonderful legacy, a legacy of love.

Their first love was for God and His Word, which guided, encouraged and supported them. Their love for the Scriptures overflowed into a passion for Bible translation. Their deep desire to see God's Word available to all people in their own language was anchored in their belief that the Word could become active, take root and change lives for eternity. Bob and Ruth also loved people…their family, their Wycliffe colleagues, and their neighbours. And theirs was a practical, hands-on love. They ministered with a Cameroonian church, reached out to prisoners, discipled young believers, taught neighbourhood Bible classes, and offered compassionate prayer and hospitality to many. Finally, Bob and Ruth's wonderful love of life led them to enjoy to the fullest every day the Lord gave them. Their zeal and energy found creative expression in sports, gardening, breeding and training dogs, hosting special events, painting and household projects. We marveled as we watched the full measure of life they poured into every day.

This book offers a rich treasury of stories, illustrations and example of faith forged in the purifying heat of trials and sufferings. For those who knew and loved Bob and Ruth, it will evoke many memories, encouraging us in our own walk with Jesus Christ and bringing forth expressions of thanksgiving for this remarkable couple and for their commitment. For those who did not know them, this book should serve as a testimony of the mighty things God can do with two lives wholly devoted to Him. All who read it will be enriched with an intimate, loving glimpse into the hearts, lives and legacy of two faithful saints. May your own faith be encouraged, your vision of God broadened, your commitment to Christ deepened, and your love for all people strengthened as you walk through these pages dedicated to two people who truly abided in their Father's heavenly love.

—*Pete Kluck*
Yaounde, Cameroon

Preface

"The ransomed of the Lord will return.
They will enter Zion with singing; everlasting joy
will crown their heads. Gladness and joy will overtake them,
and sorrow and sighing will flee away."

(Isaiah 51:11)

In Paul's Epistle to the Romans, he salutes those *"Who are loved by God and called to be saints."* He further declares, *"I thank my God through Jesus Christ for all of you, because your faith is being reported all over the world."*

Since the promotions to Glory of our son, Bob, and his wife, Ruth, on January 30, 2000, we have received messages from all parts of the world. These have not only conveyed comfort and strength, but also vivid reminders of the faith and faithfulness of our children and their influence upon so many lives.

To write, not only of their lives and deaths, but also about their example and influence has not been an easy project. But encouragement—from family and friends, from Wycliffe workers and Christian friends—has helped to strengthen our resolve to put into print, thoughts and feelings. This is the story of their dedicated lives.

The primary purpose of this publication is not only to attest to God's goodness and grace, but to bring support to others who may have known their own "valley experiences." It is hoped also that it will be a firm reminder that life is not measured by how long we live, but by what we have done for Christ during our earthly journey.

Additionally, may this publication be a challenge to young people who are grappling with the call of God in their own lives. Like Bob and Ruth, may their response be that of the prophet Isaiah, "Here am I, send me!"

To this end, we dedicate this book.

1

The Reality of Tragedy

"Do not boast about tomorrow, for you do not know what a day may bring forth."

(Proverbs 27:1)

The night of January 30th, 2000 cannot be erased from my wife's and my memories. As had been our custom, we were watching the late-night news on CTV. Dramatically and suddenly, there appeared on the screen a picture of an airplane descending into the ocean off the Ivory Coast in Western Africa. It was announced that it was a Kenyan Airline Airbus traveling from Abidjan to Nairobi, Kenya.

An e-mail received a few days previously had informed us that was the route that Bob and Ruth would be traveling that Sunday night. We quickly searched for that information and confirmed it was true. As co-directors for Wycliffe Bible

Translators for the sub-Sahara area of Africa, they had been on a two-week tour to several West African countries, conducting seminars and bringing encouragement to Wycliffe workers and their families. They had spoken of their anticipated joy at being back in their apartment in Nairobi on Monday morning.

Within minutes of the TV announcement, our telephone began to ring, providing positive information that Bob and Ruth had been taken to the airport in Abidjan that Sunday night. The sad news was quickly relayed to loved ones. A call came from our granddaughter, Erin, a student at Trinity Western University in Langley, B.C. pouring out her heart and tears. Together we prayed that her parents might be among the survivors.

It was a long night for us as we sat glued to the television, watching and waiting for some glimmer of hope. We followed the reports as they filtered through, and made contact with the Kenyan Airline office in London, England and the Canadian External Affairs in Ottawa. There was still no official confirmation that Bob and Ruth were lost. However, the next day the full impact of this tragedy reached us when it was declared that they were presumed dead.

The reality of all that had happened in the past twelve hours now struck home to us. Like a near-fatal blow, our minds went back ten-and-a-half years before. Bob and Ruth and their three children had just returned to Canada on homeland furlough. Six days later, on June 23rd, 1989, we stood in a hospital room in Hamilton, Ontario and shared the unbearable reminders of the brevity and the uncertainty of life. Our two grandchildren—Ross, aged ten, and Timothy, aged five—had both succumbed to cerebral malaria that had been picked up in Kenya on their journey home. The doctor in Hamilton had misdiagnosed their condition, stating that they had strep throat. But it was far more serious, and in two separate hospitals that Friday, they were taken to be with Jesus.

The memory of two little caskets at the front of the Salvation Army Argyle Citadel, could not be erased. The memorial service, attended by over 500 people, was both heart-rending and also a firm reminder that Ross and Timothy were now in heaven. When the Salvation Army band played "Jesus Loves Me" it brought a fresh revelation of Christ holding the children in His arms, when He was on earth, and saying "let the little children come to me..." I also remembered Bob being the first person to pray when he, with Wycliffe workers, held a vigil following that service. With him and Ruth, and family members, we struggled to reconcile this tragedy with God's plans and purposes, but resolved to leave such mysteries for heaven to reveal.

Now, these years later, we were being confronted with news of the deaths of the boy's parents. This sickening blow was almost too much for us to bear. Questions, not always audible, but nonetheless real, began to flow from our hearts. Why did this have to happen? Could God not have intervened and their flight been cancelled or missed? Turmoil in the Ivory Coast had prevented Bob and Ruth from flying into this country weeks before. Why was there peace now and their travel plans not been averted as had happened earlier?

The burden seemed too much to bear, and there was almost a declaration of "Anger against God." Surely, the promises of security, rest and long life found in Scripture should have been in evidence at this particular time. Where were the answers to this puzzle, which was so obvious to many believers and which could not be unraveled?

The sad reality of it all that happened was inescapable and far too difficult for us to handle. With our own resources, we could not survive alone. Divine intervention was the only hope for support in this time of seeming tragedy.

2

Overwhelming Reactions

"We were under great pressure, far beyond our ability to endure, so that we despaired even of life. Indeed, in our hearts we felt the sentence of death. But this happened that we might not rely on ourselves, but on God, who raises the dead."

(2 Corinthians 1:8b,9)

When tragedies happen, there is almost always an immediate response on the part of those who are suffering. This is not unusual. As finite creatures we are always wanting to know the why and the wherefore. We were no different. We were simply following in the footsteps of thousands of others who had questions to ask and answers to find.

Biblical references came to mind immediately. I had often preached on such responses and now found myself in the company of such people as Gideon who had said, "WHY has this befallen me?" Job had asked the same "WHY?" in the third chapter of his book, exactly five times. And even the Son of God, when on the cross, lifted his head toward heaven and cried, "My God, my God, WHY have you forsaken me?"

I remembered one particular sermon I had preached in Ottawa after a dear friend was taken seriously ill. I based my message on a statement from Peter Marshall—"What do you do when the raft comes apart?" It was an attempt to bring comfort and solace to a family who loved their mother dearly, and whose illness deeply affected them.

And now, at least it seemed, *our* raft was coming apart. Reactions and responses were understandable. "Why would God take two devoted persons who were engaged in missionary service and take them at the height of their ministry?" "Why were elderly persons, suffering in hospitals and nursing homes, allowed to live and others were taken in their vigorous years?" "Where was God in all of this?"

Years previously, when Bob was flying small Cessna planes in Africa, we would pray specifically for his safety. Weather conditions, unknown destinations, difficult flight runways were all hazards that were filled with danger. Protection and survival had been his in those circumstances and we had thanked God for answered prayer.

Since becoming a Director for Wycliffe, he was not allowed to pilot their planes. Sometimes, he might take the controls, but only for a brief time. He, with Ruth, was expected to take commercial flights, and leave the piloting to someone else. They had estimated in their new role that fifty percent of their time would be away from home, and plane travel would he the primary means of travel. Again, we would commit them to the Lord and ask Him to give them protection and security. Now the end of their earthly lives took place on an established airline!

There were friends who reacted as we did. They were asking questions too, and hoping to find some justification for this tragedy. One even suggested in her letter, that we now had permission to begin throwing things around our house to vent our feelings. But it wasn't that easy, and with God's help and the help of many others who came to provide us with support, we would press on to the "road to recovery." After all, we had faced devastating tragedy before, and we needed fresh support now.

In our quest for answers, we remembered when Bob and Ruth were interviewed on the Christian TV program, "100 Huntley Street," on April 13th, 1999.

David Mainse:

"Do you blame God for the deaths of your two sons?"

Ruth:

"No. One of the best books that we read as we questioned what had happened to us was probably Edith Shaeffer's book, *Affliction*. She gives an excellent illustration of two museums. And the people in each of these give praise and glory to God for two different reasons. In one museum are those who suffered and the evil one said, "If that happened, those people would lose their faith.' And God says, 'No, it won't happen that way.' And He allows something that will ultimately bring great glory to Him. And then others, God allows healing to come into their lives and that healing also brings great glory to Him. But we believe God was in total control."

Bob:

"I think our response when we faced the loss of our two sons was to embrace God. We ran to Him and said, 'We need to experience maximally what God can bring to our lives through this tragedy. We believe that He holds the world in the palm of His hands. He holds our lives as committed believers and He wants to accomplish something through this…purposefully, intentionally. And as we clung to Him for all we were worth, we began to see God's great and precious promises to us of grace poured out again and again in our desperation and our despair."

We now realized that as Bob and Ruth had accepted the deaths of their two sons, then we must do the same as we faced this further tragedy. After all, we had prayed for Bob and Ruth when we last saw them the previous July at the Toronto Pearson International Airport, as they embarked for Africa. We had committed them into God's care. Now they were in His arms, and reunited with their two sons in heaven.

A few months before his death, Bob commented on his appointment as SIL's Africa Area Director, "Trusting that God is in control, and understanding that His strength is available in the many situations where my weakness becomes evident, is probably the most important key to my being willing to do this job."

Yes, weeping and mourning would take place, but it would be tempered with the certainty that we would meet our loved ones again. This tragedy could and would be turned into triumph! And merging our weakness with His strength would be our secret for spiritual survival.

3

Enabling Grace

"When you pass through the waters, I will be with you...
When you walk through the fire, you will not be burned; the
flames will not set you ablaze."

(Isaiah 43:2)

I mmediately the word was circulated about the tragedy, our telephone began ringing, e-mails reached us, and flowers and messages came to the door of our condo. The media was pressing for information and reaction. The question most often asked was, "How are you coping in the face of this tragedy?"

In July of 1999, we had moved to Prince Albert to be close to our family. Our daughter, Carolyn, her husband, David, and their three children were very special in our lives. Providentially, we were now close to them and shared the sad news as a family. As many mentioned, God must have had a purpose in our moving from Ontario to Saskatchewan when we did.

On hearing the news, the divisional leaders for The Salvation Army in Saskatchewan, Lieutenant.-Colonels Len and Bernice McNeilly, telephoned and said they were on their way to visit us. The journey would take almost two hours, but they arrived with flowers in their hands. The McNeillys had served for a number of years in both France and Africa, and had entertained Bob and Ruth in their home in Paris when they were returning to Africa, following furlough. Our corps officers, Captains Mike and Leanne Hoeft, came and shared our grief. A special prayer meeting was convened to pray for those who had been bereaved, and members of the Army corps took turns in providing us with meals.

What a comfort to know that we were surrounded by a host of supportive people. With Bible in hand, we turned to portions of Scripture which gave us hope and uplift. We sensed immediately that we were not alone in the face of this dreadful calamity. Recognition that our loved ones were now with the Lord, and with their two boys, brought fresh hope and strength. Prayer became a focal point of all that had happened. Even with tears in our eyes, we were able to pour out our hearts to a Saviour who had also known severe suffering in His earthly life.

Wycliffe workers and Salvationists the world over were now in touch with us. It seemed that we were lifted up by prayer that came from all parts of the globe. Readily, we realized that there is no distance in prayer and the outflow of compassion and concern which was extended to us personally. As a songwriter reminds us, "Grace is flowing like a river," and we were the recipients of this in an abundant measure. With Annie Johnson Flint, we said, "He giveth more grace as our burdens grow greater."

Handling questions and comments from the media was not easy. With persistence and purpose, they were unrelenting in their attempts to assess this tragedy. Despite our difficulty in responding, God gave us immediate answers as we pointed to the faith of Bob and Ruth, and our own faith, too. We determined that, with the help of the Lord, we could survive this storm in our lives. Captain Hoeft had arranged for a meeting with television, radio and newspaper representatives at the Army's Community Centre. Here we found, again, the strong arm of the Lord giving us direction as we sought to honour the lives of our loved ones, and to give honour to the Lord We wanted to firmly remind our viewers and hearers that heaven was our ultimate destination and despite the tragedy of these hours, our faith in His plan and purpose was unwavering.

In the next days, our mailbox was filled with cards and letters, which provided us with sympathy and understanding. This sincere outpouring of love and compassion made us realize again that nothing can match the Family of God. This support came from the General (John Gowans) to the most humble soldier of Christ who wanted to remind us that we were being remembered. Tributes about Bob and Ruth were very heartwarming and a reminder that their labour for Christ had not been in vain.

We would wonder, "How do people cope in time of sorrow who do not know the Lord Jesus Christ? To whom do they turn in their time of affliction?" The family is always a great source of strength and support, but to whom, when alone, do we direct our thoughts? We were re-learning the value of knowing that "Christ Is the answer to our every need." As the Psalmist reminded us, we are to *'cast* (our) *bur-*

den upon the Lord and He will sustain (us), *and never suffer the righteous to be moved* (Psalm 55:22, RSV).

Although the waters were deep and the fire hot, we were certain that the Lord was with us through all of these experiences. The refining process was taking effect, and we were rising in the arms of the Saviour to heights where our peace could not be destroyed.

4

Canopy of Blessing

*"... unless a kernel of wheat falls to the ground and dies,
it remains only a single seed. But if it dies,
it produces many seeds."*

(John 12:24)

The belief that God has a total plan and purpose for every life is a declaration made by most Christians. To begin with, we believe that we are not on this earth by chance. The Psalmist assures us *"...the plans of the Lord stand firm forever, the purposes of His heart through all generations"* (Psalm 33:11).

To deny such a truth is to select our own future and to allow God's designs to be frustrated. As we trace the hand of the Lord on our lives, we also submit to the fact that our future is secure in His love. In relationship to this life, we believe that *"All things work together for good"* (Romans 8:28). As for the future, we are confident as the hymn writer says, *"He leadeth me O blessed thought."*

God had a desired destination for the gifts and graces of Bob and Ruth. It was His plan for them to give themselves in sacrificial service in missionary endeavour. Never once did they deny that they were on the mission field because the Lord planted them there. Even after the death of their two sons, they believed emphatically that they must return to their chosen field of service. This destiny became their primary objective when they were young soldiers of the Cross, Ruth having served as a lay-missionary in Kenya, and later in their united service overseas.

A beautiful reminder of this dedication came from one of Bob's close friends, now living in Ireland, in a letter he had written twenty-five years earlier. This is what he had said when giving thought to overseas service:

"I can't be like Christ without being a Christian. As I obey, the Holy Spirit unfolds within. I find it hard to comprehend all this richness and blessings can be mine by Christlikeness dying to self, accepting Christ as Saviour and Lord and letting His Spirit work in me. I honestly have never experienced so much peace, happiness, satisfaction… and many personal qualities that we all desire as humans. It's supernatural and it's real! I responded in faith and surrender and the progression in Christlikeness has involved watchfulness, prayer, conscious effort and intelligent co-operation i.e., the program of God. It's so great to know you can be completely fulfilled as a person and that A GREATER LIFE IS YET IN STORE FOR US WHEN WE DIE. God has been so good to me! I told you how I see God leading me into missionary service. The doors have really been opening lately…."

Bob's years at the University of Waterloo were times of development, both mentally and spiritually. Involvement with Inter-Varsity Christian Fellowship gave him opportunity to share with fellow Christians, and also to reach out to others. In a marvelous way, he was privileged to live with Pieter and Johanna Vos in the rural town of Conestoga. In their colonial home there was always fun and laughter, a Godly influence and even work with their animals. Bob became very close friends with the Vos boys.

Pieter Sr. was promoted to Glory from the Holy Land in 1997. His wife, Johanna, who joined him in heaven in March, 2001 had sent this beautiful remembrance of Bob: "I loved that boy, his faith was so real. One evening, he drove with Pieter and me. The sky got so red. Bob said, 'Perhaps the Lord is coming.' It was so natural for him to talk about the Lord, whom he really loved."

Following his graduation in Urban Planning from the university, Bob and Ruth were married in Hamilton on August 13th, 1977. My wife and I were stationed as divisional leaders in Regina, Saskatchewan, and we had the joy of journeying to Ontario to perform the ceremony. The next stage in their preparation for overseas service took them to Langley, B.C., where Bob took flight training at Trinity Western University. Enrollment at Centennial College in Toronto in Aircraft Maintenance was the next step, followed by practical work at the airport in High Level, Alberta. Several months were then spent in extensive preparation in the Jungle Aviation and Radio Service Center in Waxhaw, South Carolina.

It took seven years before their eventual journey overseas with Wycliffe, and their assignment to Cameroon; Bob as an aircraft mechanic, and Ruth as a schoolteacher and hostess.

For several months, he studied French in Switzerland. On returning to Cameroon, he became what he had long dreamed about; hands on service as a missionary pilot, before his appointment as Director for that country.

George and Alda Fletcher, who were with them in Waxhaw, sent this message following their deaths:

"Ever since the time Bob and Ruth first arrived for Bob's pilot evaluation, in 1983, we have been dear friends. I was the one who did his evaluation and orientation training. Bob was not one of our 'ace' pilots, yet he impressed all with his humility, consistency, gentlemanliness and his solid above-average piloting skills. In both Bob and Ruth's interaction with people, their godliness shone brightly. When Bob left for Cameroon, it was said here among the staff: 'He'll be one of our leaders one day.' And so it was!

"After the loss of their two boys, when in their home in Cameroon, people were impressed with the young folk who were always in and out of their home. They were parents to many. To attend church with them, one could see how the Africans respected and loved them. Their freedom in talking about the Lord drew you into their presence. When word was received of their deaths, it was a like a knife stab in the heart. Tears may be here, but there are none past the gates of their eternal home. We rejoice in the grace of our Lord who gave us Bob and Ruth.

"Without doubt, God's divine purposes for Bob and Ruth's future were fulfilled in this life. But even through their deaths, the future of others has been readily confirmed because of their faith."

Here are two of the several reminders of this happening:

1. A young person applied for service with Wycliffe in March 2000. When in Calgary, for a memorial service at the Wycliffe Canadian office, a worker shared a testimony with us. In her submission, the applicant was to tell what influenced her to serve with this missionary organization. She said, "It was the deaths of Bob and Ruth Chapman that caused me to consider what I ought to do with my life."

2. In Montreal, Quebec after reading of the tragic deaths of the Chapmans, a ninety-year-old Buddhist whose grandson was with Wycliffe overseas, was deeply moved. His grandson had been the idol of his life, following the death of his own daughter, years previously. He saw in this boy great potential in the legal field, but after receiving his degree as a lawyer, the grandson, Lui Tran, applied for missionary service. The grandfather was deeply disappointed; he had not only lost his beloved daughter but now his grandson as well.

For a long time Nam resisted Christ, but in February, 2000 things changed dramatically. The front pages of Canadian newspapers covered the fatal accident that had killed Canadians, Bob and Ruth Chapman in an airplane crash near Abidjan, West Africa. On that morning, as usual, Nam picked up the Montreal La Presse paper and read the heading, "Canadian Missionary Couple Killed in Plane Crash off the Coast of Cote d'Ivoire." He discovered that this couple served with Wycliffe Bible Translators - the same organization with which his grandson was working. Reading the story, Nam also learned that the Chapmans had lost two sons to cerebral malaria while on furlough eleven years earlier. They had nevertheless decided to return to Cameroon. This story of sacrifice and devotion deeply touched him because he too had lost two children. He imagined his grandson sitting in an airplane over Africa. What if he had been…?

The beautiful sequel to this story was that a pastor and his wife, from the local Vietnamese Protestant church, visited Nam's family to bring New Year's greetings. The pastor told him about Christ and the message of God's salvation. But unlike previous encounters, Nam seemed to be open and willing to listen. To everyone's amazement, when asked this time if he was ready to accept Christ into his life, he said, "Yes!" On February 7, 2000, his name was entered into the Lamb's book of life. And all because of the deaths of two Wycliffe workers.

Yes, the words of the Apostle Paul are true. If Bob and Ruth could now share their witness with us, they would undoubtedly say, as did Paul, in Philippians 1:12, "What has happened to me has really served to advance the gospel." Their goodness was reflected, not only in their strong commitment to overseas service and in the common things of life. These tributes honour their memory.

THE LIVES AND WORK OF BOB AND RUTH CHAPMAN:
A PHOTOGRAPHIC REMEMBRANCE.

Right:
Bob and Ruth with
Ross, Erin, and
baby Timothy
before leaving for
Cameroon
in 1983.

The Chapman family in Cameroon

Right:
Bob and Ruth with
their children, in
Yaounde, Cameroon.

Below:
The Chapmans in Switzerland, 1986.

The Chapmans with Bob's parents, in Switzerland on Ascension Day, 1986.

Erin, Timothy and Ross Chapman, Christmas 1988.

Left:
Kenyan family—
Ruth taught school
with this man.
Photo taken en
route to Canada
in 1989.

Below:
Taken by Bob up north over Christmas. Two Mofu girls of Cameroon.

Above: Bob and Ruth with the Tawe family, good friends from Faith Baptist Church

Below: Ruth at the Church Deacon's meeting.

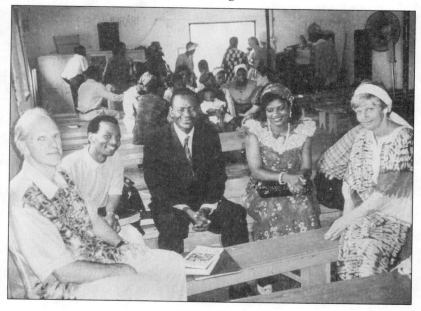

Below: Ruth Chapman surrounded by children at the dedication of the New Testament for Enagham People, December 1997 in southwestern Cameroon. Children were always a part of Ruth's ministry.

Above:
Bob receives, from a village elder, a hollowed cow horn
from which they drink at special ceremonies.

Below: Ruth at a gathering of women from the quatrier
doing their Wednesday Bible study.

Above:
Bob Chapman, when director of the Cameroon Branch, presenting a certificate to Nchio-Minkee Emmanuel, the main local translator of the New Testament for the Babungo people in northeast Cameroon.

Below:
The Chapmans at Waxhaw in South Carolina with fellow Cameroonians who work with CABTAL..

*The Yamba New Testament dedication
with translator Ginny Bradley,
as well as Ellen Jackson and Terri Scruggs.*

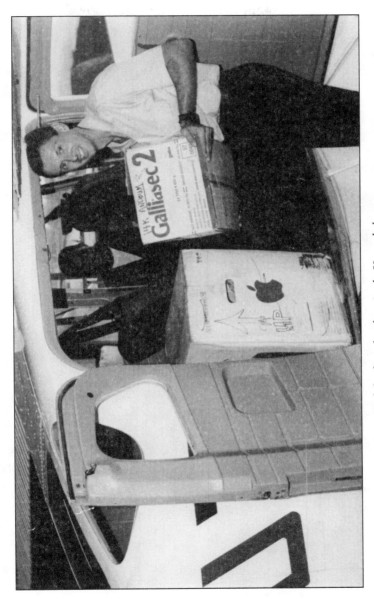

Bob loading the plane in the Yaounde hangar.

Bob and Ruth's apartment in Nairobi, Kenya.

5

Legacies of Tribute

"Think of all the good that has come from their lives.... "
(Hebrews 13:7b, NLT)

A multitude of tributes have been received regarding the influences, strong faith and selfless ministry of Bob and Ruth. They touched the lives of Wycliffe associates and the African people themselves. Their goodness was reflected in their strong commitment to overseas service, and in the common things of life. These tributes honour their memory:

"My wife, Ruth and I are Canadian missionaries serving with Wycliffe. We began in Ghana, Africa in 1982 and later worked and lived in Yaounde, Cameroon from January 1993 until January 1999.

During this time our house was only a 'stone's throw' from the Chapmans and they became our best friends. Their daughter, Erin, was the same age as our older two boys, and the kids all went to school together, and became good friends. Occasionally, we went on vacations with the Chapmans, celebrated Christmas and the Canadian Thanksgiving together. As an International Linguistics Consultant with Wycliffe, I first got to know Bob and Ruth in 1989 when I was invited to Cameroon to conduct an eight-week linguistics workshop. The Chapmans were very hospitable and invited me to their home for supper one night. Earlier that day, Ruth had given me a haircut, and as the evening progressed I got to know them better along with their three children, Ross, Erin and Tim. Imagine how shocked I was when I learned that Ross and Tim died of cerebral malaria just three short months after I had been in their home.

Though broken with grief, the Chapmans returned to Africa with renewed vigor to continue the work that God had called them to do. Bob and Ruth were very mature spiritually and emotionally. Once while Bob was our Cameroon Branch Director, our families were on vacation together at the beach near Kribi. Lying on a recliner, facing the ocean, Bob turned to me at one point and explained that they were creating a new position on the administration team and invited me to consider accepting it.

All of my career I had fought to stay out of administration, believing instead that God had called me to be a professional linguist. So I wasn't prepared to accept this invitation straight off. Bob gave me a month to think it over and at the end of the month, after praying about it, I finally told Bob that I would not be able to accept it. This was difficult for me to do, not only because Bob was my friend, but because I also knew that he himself had given up flying to go into administration.

Bob's response was a model for any administrator to follow. He listened to me without interrupting, asked a few questions when I had finished and then graciously accepted my decision. If he was disappointed in me, he never let it show nor did he let it affect our personal relationship.

We have many questions as to why the Lord allowed the Chapmans to be taken from us that will probably never be answered here on earth. Even if they were, I am not sure we would necessarily understand the reasons. During the memorial service, held in Hamilton, I reflected on these things. Who is God that He must be reduced to acting in a manner that WE consider good? Not everything I consider good is utilitarian. Sometimes I consider some things good purely for aesthetic reasons.

Perhaps God also has something that is good to Him that is as different from what we consider good as aesthetics is different from utility. We don't know. I do know, however, that He has promised in His Word, '*we know that everything works together for the good of those who love God and are called according to His purpose for them*' (Romans 8:28, NLT). And in that we take great comfort!"

—Dr. Keith Snider,
an international linguistics consultant,
now on staff at the Linguistic Center
at Trinity Western University
in Langley, B.C. Canada.

The following were shared at the memorial service in Hamilton, Ontario on Feb. 12, 2000.

"Mom, you were the most amazing person I ever met. You were such a strong Godly woman. You always seemed to know exactly what I needed to hear and always had a Bible verse to go with it. When I was younger it bothered me that you always had to throw God into everything, but as I grew up, that was something I respected so much, You must have had the whole Bible memorized. I remember your comforting touch. When I was sick you were the one who made me feel better. I remember the way you wanted to know so much about me, always willing to listen to anything I had to say no matter how unimportant it was. Now Mom, I wonder who will take your place? You were so giving, giving up your spare time to drive me places, cutting someone's hair or checking a prayer letter. There never seemed to be a limit as to how far you would go for me. Mom, you can't imagine how much I cherish our time together last October. These last few days were so wonderful.

"Daddy, oh Daddy, where can I start? You always knew how to make me smile no matter how hard I tried to be angry at you it never worked. You were so dedicated to your job, wanting so badly for all to have God's Word. And Daddy, who else would have shared my love of dogs. I'll always remember those walks with you and the dogs early in the morning. The times when I was sick and you would come home from work and give me a big kiss and ask if I needed anything even after you had a rough day at work. Daddy, you were such a romantic husband. Always doing special things for Mom; always making sure no day went by without her knowing how much you loved her. The way you spoiled her every year on your anniversary weekend away. But most of all, Daddy, I remember how ready you were to show you loved me. Remember, Daddy, you came home from a hard days' work and I was crying. You asked me why and I told you my shoes for the banquet were nicked. You stayed up until four in the morning that night fixing them for me.

"Mommy and Daddy, I wonder more and more each day what I will do without you. There are so many times I cry when I think of you and the boys in heaven. And then I think of you Mom with Timothy on your lap and you Dad with Ross and I know you are always here with me. I know that one of you would have chosen to stay with me if you could have but God knows, and I am so glad that you are all just waiting for me to join you."

—*Daughter, Erin*

"Ruth was a wonderful sister and my best friend. Even though, since her marriage in 1977, we were usually separated by thousands of miles, we remained very close. We were both faithful letter writers which kept us involved in each other's often very different lives.

"God blessed Ruth and me with great parents who provided a warm and loving Christian home. As young kids, we had the usual squabbles which I always won because I was bigger. As teens we got along quite well, except when we played piano duets. Practice sessions sometimes involved arguing over what we would play, how fast we would play it, which part we would play and who was hogging the piano bench. We usually ended up laughing over it.

"Ruth was able to develop and maintain meaningful relationships with people wherever she went. A letter she wrote from Cameroon last month mentioned how many people they were able to connect with, sometimes having two suppers in one night, so as to see everyone. Bob and Ruth had a fantastic marriage and shared a goal of missionary endeavour, spending years in training and preparation for it.

"There were many comings and goings but they never

became routine. It was always hard to say 'goodbye.' But this time is by far the most difficult. Their journey on earth is over, far earlier than we had hoped. This journey has been successful and they have now seen God. Even in times of terrible trial and sorrow they remained steadfast and showed, by their return to Cameroon after Ross and Tim died, that following God's will is more important than anything else. We take comfort in knowing that they died doing what they loved. We don't understand why their ministry was stopped, seemingly in mid-stream. But God is sovereign and we hold on to the promise that 'All things work together for good…'"

—*Sylvia, Ruth's sister*

"I first met Ruth in 1968 when I moved to Hamilton to attend McMaster University.

"We quickly developed a very special relationship which has continue over these thirty two years; kept alive by personal visits when possible, but mainly by letter. Ruth has had and will continue to have a profound impact on my life.

"As I have been re-reading her letters these past ten days, it seems to me that they reflect three of the main priorities of Ruth's life; her relationship with God, the living out of her calling and her family. Her first concern has always been her love for God and the ways in which she could nurture that relationship. Whatever she heard or read, she always applied that to herself, calling herself to live more deeply in the Lord. She often shared what she was reading in the Scriptures and how it was speaking to her. I deeply admired her disciplined prayer life.

"Secondly, she always lived out a sense of her calling, reaching out to people, listening to them, and loving them. That calling was expressed in making use of every minute before and after the meetings at the Argyle Corps to talk with people. When Ruth and I got together she made very sure that she listened to what was going on in my life just as much as I listened to her. In thirty two years of friendship, she never forgot my birthday, no matter where she has been. She wrote hundreds of letters to people in the cracks of time, riding in cars, trains and even airplanes. Her letters to us are now a wonderful legacy.

"Thirdly, Ruth talked and wrote about her family. She was a devoted mother to Ross, Timothy and Erin. She wrote frequently about her desire to see Erin settled and happy. She told me she coped with the distance between them by focusing not on how much she missed Erin, but how much she loved and appreciated her.

"I will deeply miss Ruth; her letters, her encouragement, her life that challenged me to live closer to God. But their impact on us will continue. God's kingdom has been extended by their lives. and they would want us to continue that work and to trust Him, even in the most difficult of times."
—*Major Cathie Harris, Toronto*

"I got to know Bob in 1973 when he was introduced to our family. Through the keen insight of his parents (to whom we are forever grateful), our home became Bob's home away from home for the four years that he attended the University of Waterloo.

"Bob was a person who loved life, and who enjoyed being in the company of people, evidenced by his popularity among his peers, either at school or in his Salvation Army family. This was apparent to everyone who knew Bob that he enjoyed being a member of God's family and was certain of his salvation. He was very disciplined in his studies and in his devotional life. The experiences of an overseas short term mission to Haiti, his attendance at the Salvation Army Candidates' Seminar, and his studies at Emmanuel Bible College were the beginning of his preparation by God for his eventual call as a pilot to overseas missions.

"Bob's faith was solid as a result of working diligently and becoming knowledgeable in the Scriptures, applying them to his daily living. His life was a continual witness of his Christian beliefs and principles. He loved the challenge of a good debate on any topic, especially if it related to theology, traditional worship or morality.

"Over the years, it was thrilling to hear Bob and Ruth speak with such excitement and zeal about their work such as being present when the Scriptures were placed in the hands of tribal communities for the first time. They pursued their work with the assurance that they were right where God wanted them regardless of many challenges.

"There is no doubt that according to God's command as the physical dross fell away, God's angels bore Bob and Ruth up in their hands lest they dash their feet against any harm, carrying them immediately into the presence of the Lord. This was the goal and the glorious prize for which they laboured in love here on earth. *We have sorrow now, but we will see you again! and our hearts will rejoice.*" (John 16:22)

—*John Vos, Kitchener, Ontario*

Other tributes—many from "The Leaf," a Wycliffe Bible Translators publication—were shared. These were compiled by Janet Seevers of Wycliffe Canada:

"We deeply mourn the loss of Bob and Ruth Chapman, and announce the news of their deaths with great sadness and sorrow. They were dear friends and colleagues. Bob started in the role of Africa area director of Wycliffe in June of 1999. Ruth assisted him in this role. They made a vigorous start over the past six months. We anticipated their significant contributions to the work of Bible translation efforts in Africa. Their deaths are a tremendous loss to the organization and to each of us personally. The challenge will be great to find the person to follow Bob in this leadership role."

> —*Dr. John Watters, Executive Director,*
> *Wycliffe Bible Translators International.*

From Julie Staples: Ruth sent me this e-mail on April 13, 1999. Julie, a nurse in Cameroon, had told her about a co-worker who recovered after being extremely ill from malaria "We really like the way the Bermudians put it, when we were there a week ago. They started their service with the leader saying, "God is good" and the congregation replying "all the time," before the leader again said, "God is good." So our God is great because He heals malaria and our God is great because He can overcome even a lethal number of malaria parasites, and our God is great because His mercies are new every morning even when the healing doesn't occur, and great is His faithfulness."

Julie responded the next day: "I want you to know that the miracle of grace, that I have witnessed in your life, has impacted my life more deeply than any other miracle I've seen the Lord perform. Healing is a wonder, and brings great glory to the Lord. But your lives, your love for the Lord, your steadfast belief in His goodness, in spite of the tremendous pain He allowed in your lives speaks to me so much more of the miraculous power of God in our lives, working to make us into those who are more than conquerors in Christ. You and Bob have such an inspiration to me through the years."

"A while back Ruth sent me a letter. In it she posed a question that she had been dealing with, which I have tried to keep before me as well. It was this: 'What am I becoming?' Before the accident I would have thought that Ruth was becoming more and more like Jesus. I would have been right. Now, as I reflect on my memory of her, I see her more as John, pointing the way for us. Or like Paul, encouraging us all to be imitators of Christ, to press on, toward the goal, for the prize of our upward call. I can see her even now, smiling, encouraging us to press on."

—*Deborah Crough, WBT Canada*

"Bob and Ruth lived in the Word, I never knew anyone to be so consistently and unselfconsciously immersed in prayer and study of the Bible. They were not perfect, we all knew that, but they were committed to following the Lord's path wherever it took them. They also loved and relied on each other a great deal; they were obviously good friends as well as spouses."

—*Barbara Trudell, Africa Area*

"What comes primarily to my mind is their servant heart, which was demonstrated by their devoted ministry to members and to many Cameroonians. They had at one time or the other all Cameroonian branch members over for dinner. Nearly every day they would invite somebody to their home for a meal."

—*Martin Engeler, WBT Canada*

"Their emphasis on prayer and on seeking the Lord in all things helped all of us through branch crises that arose, and helped us to be unified on issues that could have been very divisive. We all appreciated their personal concern for us, and especially that we might be walking closely with the Lord."

—*Judy Hollingsworth,*
translator for the Mofu-Gudur people of Cameroon

"I want to say how deeply shocked I am to have received information on Bob and Ruth's deaths. That such gems should be taken so suddenly and so soon, while other rougher diamonds remain, can only be explained in terms of the Lord's sovereignty. Perhaps He had done all the polishing on them that he needed to do. I shall certainly miss their presence at retreats. I know many others will miss them in a multitude of ways."

—*Peter Kingston, WBT U.K.*

"How many of us have undergone such a school of suffering as Bob and Ruth, in the loss of their two boys? I never knew the boys, but over the years I have on many occasions tried to grasp the devastation which could well have engulfed Bob and Ruth when they lost one son, and then the other. But they came through triumphantly and the experience gave them a deep understanding of the human condition and a great strength, a strength which equipped them to widen the scope of their ministry to encompass the whole of Africa!"

—*Willie Kinnaird, Cameroon*

"SIL's Cameroonian cook Robert was at market on the day after the crash, buying tomatoes. 'What's wrong with you?' asked the vendor, 'Why are you so sad?' 'My former director was just killed in a plane crash near Abidjan,' he replied. A man standing nearby spoke sharply, 'What's his name?' When Robert told him, he burst into sobs. 'He used to visit me in prison and he would bring me food there.' Chapmans began a prison ministry that prepared the way for many Cameroonians to become involved."

—*Carrie Taylor, Cameroon*

"Today is Easter Sunday. We kept to our tradition of having a sunrise service on the steps of RFIS followed by a light breakfast of hot cross buns. This was something Ruth always organized when they were still here. This evening as a branch we viewed the video of the service in Hamilton. I viewed it with increasingly mixed emotions. On one hand the ripping pain of the reality of separation was setting in. I've just spent the last hour after the service, walking around the center with Wendy Myers talking and weeping."

—*Margaret Dobson, Cameroon*

"Although we know that Bob and Ruth have been promoted to Glory and are again with Ross and Tim, and especially with Jesus, the sense of loss is still indescribable. Bob and Ruth were very special to me. My first meal ever in Cameroon was at their house! I had just arrived in Yaounde for the Africa Orientation Course and probably because I was a fellow Canadian, Ruth met me and brought me back to their home for breakfast. When I came back to Cameroon from furlough in 1992, I saw Bob and Ruth in the dining hall. I ran up to them, gave them both a big hug and said, "You came back!" The fact they did come back touched people's hearts more than one can ever imagine."

—*Larry Sequin, Cameroon*

"It is difficult to understand God's timing and His ways some times along life's path. I was in Nairobi producing a video for our national banquet tour about a week prior to the airplane crash. During that time, I had the pleasure of meeting Bob and Ruth as the three of us enjoyed a relaxed meal. Bob took time out of his busy schedule to participate in the video project by sharing his love for God's Word through a personal interview. We have now finished the video project and have dedicated the entire national Wycliffe Associates banquet tour in honour of Bob and Ruth. By the time this tour finishes, we will have hosted more than 1,300 banquets and more than 45,000 people will have their hearts challenged."

—Tedd Sutton, Orange, California

"We can hardly believe that two such wonderful people have been taken from us. We are members of the Bob and Ruth Chapman 'fan club.' From the time we first met them in Charlotte, North Carolina when they were at Waxhaw, we were impressed and challenged by their commitment to their mission in Africa and by their Christ-like spirits. We now feel as if a very important brother and sister of our family of Christ have been taken from us. The loss is a sharp pain. We want you to know that Bob and Ruth had a deep influence on our lives and that we are better persons for knowing them."

—Colonels Phil and Keitha Needham,
Rancho Palos Verdes, California

"Bob and Ruth Chapman were special colleagues and friends of mine in Cameroon. I worked closely with them as Personnel Director from 94-98. I was looking forward to Bob being my boss again when I returned to Africa in May; this time he would be Africa Area Director and I would be reporting to him from my service on the Mobile Member Care Team. I now ask, 'Why would the Lord take them?' It makes no sense to me in terms of Wycliffe SIL. They loved Africa and were so suited for this role. I really enjoyed working with them and anticipated many more years of doing so. When in Cameroon, I used to go to their place late in the evening to talk things over. Just to share, to pray and to laugh and to be together was what I needed. The load was too much alone. I always felt lighter in heart as I walked back home under the starlit sky. But I wouldn't wish them back. They loved the Lord so much and now they are with Him. Can't even imagine that. Such fullness, such joy! I was privileged to walk with them as they earnestly pressed on towards the prize, disciplined themselves, let go of things that entangled them, and faced the Cross for the joy beyond."

—Darlene Jerome, The Ivory Coast

"Bob and I met in 1991 when Faith Baptist Church was still a mobile church. By then we were worshipping in a wooden structure behind Kondengui Prison. In 1992, Bob called me to join hands with him in the Prison Ministry. There were just three of us; Enoh John, Bob and myself. The vision of Prison Ministry came through the person of Bob and when he called me, I did not hesitate, I also caught the vision. It was Bob who saw that food was a vital need for the ministry. Bob was a man full of compassion. His compassion sometimes swelled into tears. He looked at the prisoners with a lot of pity. Bob was the one who prepared all Bible study lessons. He defined the structure of the group in prison. He equally provided medical assistance to some brothers in the group. Later, through the influence of Bob, Hope Service Clinic joined the ministry to administer medical assistance to sick prisoners. For me, a true friend is a gift from God. Bob was a real friend. His concern for me was great. Bob and Ruth were my treasure. They supported me financially. They helped to pay my school fees. They stood by me when my father died. Because of them, the prison ministry continues and many have gone to their home as trophies of God."

—*Changwan Emmanuel, Cameroon*

"Bob Chapman remains for eternity as a pillar to the development of Cameroon National languages. During his tenure as Director of SIL in Cameroon, he singled out himself as a modest, humble, committed and zealous missionary and administrator. He performed his duties with practical examples and at every step strived for perfection. As such, accompanied by Ruth, he toured all the nooks and crannies of Cameroon. He attended ceremonies destined for the inauguration of mother tongue learning and launching of the translated New Testaments of the Bible. In December, 1995 Bob and Ruth defied the dusty and rough road leading to Oku and showered their blessings on the Oku Language Society. Henceforth the Oku language has developed and grown from strength to strength. The seed sown has borne enormous fruits. The Oku people prodding use their language as the main medium of communication in the Oku rural Radio Station."

—*Kendemeh Emmanual Gwani, Cameroon*

"Your untimely deaths to me was more than bearable. Your deaths created a deep bleeding wound in my heart. Your regular Godly message to us in prison broadened our spiritual knowledge but sadly today you are no more, because of the plane crash. I loved you so much, but God whose decision is final, loved you most and has called you to eternal rest."

—Njakoy Charles in Kondengui Prison

"I was Bob's secretary for four years while he was the Director of the Cameroon Branch. Not only was he my 'boss' but he and Ruth were my good friends and mentors. They truly helped me to see potential in myself that I never knew existed. They encouraged me to 'be all that I could be' by God's grace. I know that a lot of people are quoting 'God does all things well' and He does, and Bob and Ruth did use that quote often. However, my most vivid recollection of Bob is that of him bouncing in the office and when asked how he was he would respond, 'moving on by future grace.' He truly believed and lived the statement that 'the grace of the same God that has brought us this far will carry us on.' It might not feel like it and it might not always be fun (probably won't be), but you can bank on God's future grace to carry us on. As I write this, I am encouraged once again to move on by His future grace!"

—Gail Boemker, Orlando, Florida.

"Bob Chapman was a very passionate, committed person, he was appreciated quite a lot by our students. They considered him an example to model their lives after."

—Guy Saffold, Vice President,
Trinity Western University

6

Resilient in Service

"... though now for a little while you may have had to suffer grief in all kinds of trials. These have come so that your faith... of greater worth than gold, which perishes even though refined by fire... may be proved genuine and may result in praise, glory and honor when Jesus Christ is revealed."

(1 Peter 1:6b,7)

My husband and I first met the Chapman family on July 4th, 1985 in Cameroon. Our first meal there was in their home, not too surprising. Later we discovered they were always inviting people into their home for meals.

I looked up from my aged pages and remembered just how many meals we shared with them. Their dog, 'Simba' would bring things to Bob on command. It was truly amazing to the missionary wives how Ruth could do it all. She seemed superhuman in her organizational skills and in her energy. If you even attempted to keep up with Ruth's daily pace of life, you would be huffing and puffing by the end of every day. I look back now and see that God gave Bob and Ruth an uncanny ability to pack overwhelming amounts of activity and ministry into one day, perhaps this was because their lives were to be cut short.

I was first introduced to Ruth and her new baby, Timothy, by our mutual friend, Margie Johnston, when we were visiting Waxhaw's Jungle Aviation and Radio Service Center in South Carolina. Ruth's soft-spoken, gentle depth attracted me to her, and we did indeed become very close friends. We intimately shared our hearts over the fifteen years of service in Cameroon. I remember that for awhile we would fast and pray together every Monday. I remember crying to her one morning in the parking lot of our administrative center. I really didn't think I could manage staying in Cameroon. Life was just too stressful. I was at the end of my endurance. Ruth assured me that God's grace had brought me and would keep me going. She was right. That was also her message of encouragement to many other women in the Cameroon Branch, both married and single. She helped convince us of that sufficient grace.

I eventually did get over my fear of driving in Yaounde, after living there for three years. But I am very thankful for all those shopping trips downtown with Ruth. We would always stop midmorning for a pastry and a drink (grocery shopping in capital city of Cameroon took ALL morning). Ruth always asked me very probing questions and I believe the Lord used here to help me grow in my walk with Jesus.

Ruth taught kindergarten the last year before her boys died. When they returned to Cameroon in 1991, she came back to teach French and later English at our SIL high school, Rain Forest International School. She enjoyed teaching and challenging the students in their faith. Bob and Ruth's mission and motivation was Bible translation. Their third bedroom was usually occupied by a teenaged child of a village team who had to live and go to school in Yaounde, away from their parents. Instead of dwelling on the loss of their two boys, they brought in students to give them a substitute home and to make it possible for the translators to stay in the village.

Erin is an amazing combination of both Bob and Ruth. Bob's dark hair and eyes, as well as his mischievous, fun-loving personality, are knit together with Ruth's pensive and yet very open and frank approach to people. Erin was loved deeply by her "Mommy" and "Daddy," as she affectionately called them. We knew this because many times over coffee in the evenings, Paul and I, and Bob and Ruth would discuss and pray for our children.

Bob and Ruth's homegoing is a great loss to the cause of Bible translation and literacy. Their untiring energy and service was an inspiration to each of us who knew and loved them. They were untiring in serving us, their "family" in Cameroon, through aviation, teaching, hospitality, music, hair-cutting, administration and in friendship and prayer. We deeply and strongly miss Bob and Ruth, but we know where they are. They are in His glorious presence and we, too, will one day be there!

My husband, Paul, was honoured to bring the message at the funeral service for Ross and Timothy in Hamilton, Ontario, on June 27th, 1989 and here is part of what he said:

"I worked with Bob nearly every day. I appreciated his skills as a pilot and as a mechanic, but what impressed me most was his love for the Lord and the practical ways that was manifested in kindness to others, in his strong commitment to their local church, and in his commitment to his family. Often he would bring the children to the hangar.

"We knew the Chapman family pretty well. We've gone on several vacations with them, and usually spent New Year's Day together. I'd like to share something of what Ross and Timothy were like. Bob and Ruth asked me to say a little about them. They did not ask me to say anything about themselves.

"Ross adored his dad. He was always talking about what his dad could do. He was loyal to his sister, Erin, sticking up for her on the playground. You see, our daughter was in his class, that's how I know this. He was fun-loving and somewhat of a clown. He loved music, played the cornet and brought Christian music tapes for his class to hear. He was artistic and liked to draw. Just before leaving Cameroon, he won the science fair. He was competitive, playing on the junior soccer team, and he loved animals just like his dad.

"Ross could speak French well. He loved the Lord and was quick to talk about Him to his friends. He was an avid reader. He also was quick to share his bike and was specially kind to kids who were younger than him and who were easily overlooked.

"Timothy was a gentle, peace-loving kid, who didn't like conflicts. If he and his friends didn't see eye-to-eye he would just disappear rather than cause a scene. He loved to play with Lego and make ships. He loved to swim, and shared his bike easily.

"How can we explain or understand that Ross and Timothy's homegoing was an exercise of God's kindness or His justice? Perhaps we can't right now. The Apostle Paul reminds us, in 1 Corinthians 13:9,12,

> *"For we know in part; now we see but a poor reflection; then we shall see face to face. Now I know in part...then I shall know fully, even as I am fully known"*

We will miss Ross and Timothy, but we know where they are—they are in His glorious presence, and we too, will soon be there."

—*Deb Haken,*
Hershey, Pennsylvania

7

Inspirational Logbook

"… how shall they hear without someone preaching to them?
And how can they preach unless they are sent?"
(Romans 10:14,15)

Bob Chapman Jr. did not receive formal training in preaching. In his teen years, as a member of a teen-age Bible study group, he would give brief talks, but nothing too extensive. Frequently Bob would publicly share what God was doing in his life, and his determination to be a good follower of the Lord. Every New Year, he would take a specific text from the Bible as his motto for the coming year.

When at Waterloo University, he took classes at Emmanuel Bible College, under the tutelage of the Principal, Dr. Charles Seidenspinner, a powerful exponent of the Word of God and a dear friend of our family.

Bob, with Ruth, would lead Bible classes for young adults, which meant they must delve deeply into the Scriptures. Reading Christian books was a passion for both of them, even up to the time of their deaths.

It seemed for Bob that preaching became a special gift from the Lord. In preparing his messages, he would spend many hours at the typewriter (later the computer). Prayer would precede everything and the Holy Spirit was the author of what he wrote. I can still picture him at the computer, agonizing over the message which he believed the Lord had given him. All of his sermons contained texts from the Bible. Statements and admonitions were confirmed, for without the Spirit interpreting the message, he knew it would be fruitless and meaningless.

Both he and Ruth would share the platform and pulpit together. Often, one of them would describe a missionary episode of courage and sacrifice, and the other would preach the sermon. Prayer was the focal point as they shared their messages with the people and as they spoke of their work. They loved Wycliffe, and felt implicitly that the Lord had led them in the footsteps of people like Cameron Townsend, the founder of this organization, and other great saints of God. For them, Bible translation was a priority and the Gospel must reach all languages and people.

In their memory are dedicated these messages which were found in a looseleaf book in their residence in Nairobi when our daughter Carolyn and her husband David, as well as Erin, went there following Bob and Ruth's death. Its pages are replete with sermon notes from Bob's personal preparation, and some that he heard from gifted speakers. In his own distinctive handwriting they were recorded, not just for time, but for eternity.

Students of homiletics might say that the structure and patterns of these messages are unorthodox. To them we would say, *"God was pleased through the foolishness of what was preached to save those who believe"* (1 Corinthians 1:21b).

THOUGHTS ON SUFFERING

1 God will not let His children to be tested in any given day beyond what His mercy will that day sustain.

2. New every morning are His compassions—Great is His Faithfulness.

3. Faithful is He who called you, He will act (1 Thessalonians 5:24).

Psalm 121: 2, 3

1. Help from the Lord—He will not let your foot slip. The One who helps you never sleeps! He stays up all night; He works for us. "For those who wait for Him" (Isaiah 64:4).

2. The Son of man came to serve (Mark 10:45). He came to strengthen (Philippians 4:13).

3. In these things we can rejoice always (Philippians 4:4); give thanks for everything (Ephesians 5:20); have peace that passes understanding (Philippians 4:7). We are to be anxious for nothing (Philippians 4:6).

Psalm 63: 1, 2 (An Embracing God)

1. "Oh God, I seek You, my soul thirsts for You, my flesh faints for You in a dry and thirsty land."—Philippians 1:21—Life in Christ, to die is gain.

Why?

1. Done with sin and disappointment.

2. Relieved of the pain of this world—a great reversal.

3. There is a profound rest.

4. "At homeness" (2 Corinthians 5:8), "Absent from the

body and at home..." True contentment.

5. With Christ, the most wonderful Person; where there is peace and joy.

The significance of reading the Word

1. We must be people of the Word; it gives meaning and power.

2. Jesus has already settled the great issues (Matthew 21:16; 21:42).

3 Paul gives solemn insistence on its need in our lives (2 Corinthians 1:13; Ephesians 3:4; 1 Thessalonians 5:27).

4. We need regular training of the mind.

5. We need direct access to God's Word.

Keeping on despite suffering

1. No self-pity! (Psalm 126: 5,6). Sown in tears, brings eventual joy and harvest.

2. A farmer must move forward, despite discouragement. His work must continue.

3. Sowing will bring us ultimate harvest. The work will not be in vain.

4. Life is filled with stress and strain; why think only of your comfort and an easy life?

The Word demands urgency

1. His Word will not return void (2 Thessalonians 3:2, Isaiah 55:11).

2. Our prayers are the means that God has appointed to do what He certainly will do. We are to finish the great commission and establish His Kingdom! To love

His appearing is to pray passionately. Pray as soldiers sharing in the battle.

If only; hurt, loss, disappointment, anger seem to need a place to fix the blame, so as to deny your true feelings. There is no need to become your own worst enemy; to sentence yourself for others to more suffering. If death is what it seems to be and life beyond is true, then we have begun a new adventure. Don't feel resentful if you must suffer. Don't feel cheated for "There is no guilt on heaven's side of death, why on this side?" There is danger in self-pity; in continuing in grief into a state of being the helpless victim. Temptation to stay in the middle of suffering. Do you really want to get well? Time is a great healer, but you must decide. You have a choice and you must exert your will. What is the connection between grief and the ills of our society? Never facing or resolving your grief or trauma leads to alcoholism, divorce, emotional problems, nervous breakdowns and even suicide. Tendency for us to blame our failures, our action and responses in our grief.

How do we handle sorrow?

You have to talk and people have to listen. Acknowledge that there will be a point of decision which will help you to overcome; to embrace God; to say how you are getting through. To decide that this situation is not going to be wasted. Our culture imposes some so-called vague rules upon us and we seldom question their validity. e.g. The length of time for grief and mourning. The value of distractions and amusements. Better not to talk about it. Be careful of your tears in public. Comments such as, "Your loved ones are better off where they are," "You just have to..." "God knows best," "In time you will forget," "Why did it have to happen?"

Our work as God's people gets validated in the details. People are watching to see if we stay at our post. Although immersed in tears, we are filled with deep joy (2 Corinthians 6:3), (Philippians 1:29). There is more in this life than just trusting in Christ; there is also a measure of suffering for Him, and the suffering is as much a gift as the trusting!

Why are we so anxious to get God off the hook when we suffer?

Paul describes suffering as a gift from God (Philippians 1:29). Peter spoke of it as God's will (1 Peter 1:7, 4:19). James reminds us (4:13) "If the Lord wills we will do this or that." Hebrews reminds us (12: 4–6) that it is His plan for our holiness. Jesus embraced such a plan in His life.

There are six reasons why God appoints suffering for His servants:

1. The objective is deeper faith and holiness.

2. Suffering endured means the reward of our experiences of God's glory increases in heaven.

3. God uses the suffering of His people (missionaries) to awaken others out of their slumber and indifference. It makes them bold and willing to take risks.

4. The suffering of Christ's messengers ministers to those they are trying to reach and may open them to the gospel (1 Thessalonians 1: 5,6).

5. The suffering of the Church is used by God to reposition the missionary troops in places they might not have otherwise gone. The book of Acts is replete in such examples. God uses upheaval and displacement and death to advance His cause.

6. The supremacy of Christ is manifest in suffering. We magnify His power and sufficiency.

The supremacy of God runs through all of these reasons. Suffering with joy proves to the world that our treasure is in heaven and not on the earth, and that the treasure is greater than anything the world has to offer. The supremacy of God's worth shines through the pain that His people will gladly bear for His name.

As the Christian writer, Piper has written, "The goal of our mission is that people from all nations will worship the True God. But worship means cherishing the preciousness of God above all else, including life itself. It is very hard to bring the nations to God from a lifestyle that communicates the love of things. So God ordains in the lives of His messengers that suffering serves our bondage to the world. When joy and love survive this we are fit to say to the nations with authenticity and power—Hope in God!"

HEZEKIAH: A MAN OF CHARACTER

(A message given at The Salvation Army Southmount Citadel Vancouver, on September 17, 1998)

"Not by might, not by power, but by my Spirit says the Lord."
(Zechariah 4:6)

What were the characteristics of this man:

1. He chose the right motives (2 Kings 18:3). Link with Matthew 6:33.

2. He put things in their right place. No compromise, nothing false in his life (2 Kings 18:4). Link with Matthew 6:24.

3. He had confidence in the right Person. (2 Kings 18:5). In whom do you put your trust? "Trust in the Lord with all your heart."

4. He called things by their right name (2 Kings 18:4). e.g. The word for snake was "Nehushtan" meaning unclean.

5. He walked in the right place and kept the commands of God (2 Kings 18:6). Are you walking rightly? Watch out for the dangers and roadblocks.

6. He had the right source of strength (2 Kings 18:7). We need freedom from our sin and our addictions.

7. He had real success; there was only one God in his life (2 Kings 18:8).

Note:

1. Hezekiah spread his letter before the Lord in the Temple. He took the necessary action (2 Kings 19:4). God must be consulted in the face of danger. Faith replaces fear.

2. He had a sense of the vindication of God's ways in dealing with the people.

3. God's response came in confirmation and protection (2 Kings 19:34).

4. He knew the need of being responsible for the people as their leader.

Leadership is a costly process. There is no guarantee against reaction, ridicule and retribution. But one man with God is always a majority. Power to be His chosen person does not come naturally, the Spirit is the One who controls, motivates and empowers.

GOD'S CHOSEN

(A devotional given in Cameroon just before Bob and Ruth were promoted to Glory)

Read: 1 Samuel 16: 1–13

Samuel was likely a thick, sturdy, strong man with long white hair and a beard flowing every which way. He had a task to perform before he took leave of this life The selection of a replacement for Saul, Israel's first king, was his mandate.

Heading to Bethlehem, Samuel probably walked a confident and steady pace; the kind that shows you are bent on a mission and know exactly what your destiny must be. No doubt people saw him coming and ran into the town to announce the news that soon a legend of that day was to arrive. The elders of the town were afraid (verse 4). This prophet was not known for just dropping in for a chat. "Have we sinned?" might have been the reaction of some. Their fears soon left when Samuel spoke the word, "Shalom," and prepared to have a community-wide worship service, which included Jesse and his sons.

It is difficult to know whether the people really paid much attention to what happened next. Samuel proceeded to examine and interview each of the sons of Jesse, one at a time. Eliab was the eldest, probably a muscular kind of man who would command respect. But he was not the man that God had chosen. The Lord told Samuel,

Do not consider his appearance or his height, for I have rejected him. The Lord does not look at the things man looks at. Man looks at the outward appearance, but the Lord looks at the heart (verse 7).

Then there was Abinadab. Possibly he was the influential brother who spoke big words and made people feel inferior because of his learning. But Samuel then dismissed him. Then came Shammah, and Samuel told Jesse the Lord had not chosen him either.

The rest of the sons are not named and Samuel had to ask, "Are these all you have?" Perhaps he was confused, wondering if he had heard God correctly and was in the right place. Was he really supposed to find the next king in Bethlehem?

The youngest son now enters the scene. He is the baby brother who isn't even called by his name. The Hebrew word for David implies insignificance, the runt of the family. David was out in the fields performing the least demanding job, baby-sitting the sheep. Surely, the Lord would not choose him to be the next king of Israel.

Often we are guilty of searching for leaders who are powerful, those who are experts and professionals, those cunning of mind as the people to look for, instead of recognizing those who are among us as the ones God is calling.

This story reminds us that God is really looking for competence in faith, in praying, in loving and giving, in patience and hope. It is a message of how God purpose includes the ordinary people. It might even be those lacking in social graces or recognition that God wants to choose and anoint for His service.

I was recently struck by the story of an Ethiopian named Wandaro. He was a youth from the southern hills and a Wolaytos by birth. One day on his way to market he took shelter in a recently erected small building. A white man approached him and asked if he could read to him from a special book. Surprisingly, Wandaro remembered an old prophecy by an Ethiopian prophet called Asa. It was about a foreigner who would bring a book telling about a Creator, whom the people would worship instead of Satan.

The next week, Wandaro returned to hear more and announced, "I renounce Satan to follow Jesus." For the first time he felt real joy in his life. He learned to read the 255 characters of the Amhane alphabet and became an enthusiast for Christ, building a church and trusting the Lord despite the death of his child and his wife deserting him.

Wandaro had encountered an Ethiopian slave-trader with the Gospel and helped him to believe. During this time Wandaro endured communist persecution, and the missionaries had to flee his city, leaving behind forty-eight believers. The enemies of the gospel burned churches, captured Wandaro and tied him in the village center and viciously beat him. He and fellow believers met secretly, and hid their Scriptures but continued to witness publicly for the Lord.

For three hours he was flogged and thrown into a bamboo prison. But with prayer and faith, he survived for a year, and when released, the first thing he did was to gather the believers together. He had a price put on his head, and was forced into seclusion. Finally, when the missionaries were able to return to the country, the Ethiopian Christians came out to greet them. The number now was not just forty-eight, but ten thousand with over one hundred established churches. All this happened because a so-called insignificant person called, Wandaro, found the Saviour and made Christ foremost in his life.

David was the youngest and the one least expected to become king. But when he left the field and stood before Samuel, the Lord said, *"Rise and anoint him, the one"* (verse 12). And verse 13 tells us, *"From that day on the Spirit of the Lord came upon David in power."* Later in chapter 17 we find him fighting against Goliath. Here was a boy facing a Philistine giant. But despite the differences in size and power, we also see an anointed servant of the Lord who believed emphatically that he was called by God to fight against the enemy. He announced to Goliath,

"You come against me with sword and spear and javelin, but I come against you in the name of the Lord Almighty, the God of the armies of Israel, whom you have defied" (verse 45).

In our imagination we see David kneeling at the brook picking up five smooth stones for his sling shot. He was in a place he had never been before, preparing to fight a war he had never fought before, and against a giant he had never seen before. The onlookers made fun of him, but this did not deter him from his task. He was modest and yet bold enough to use his sling as he knelt to select some stones from the water.

Someone has said, "The way we do our work is as important as the work we do." David kneeling at the brook becomes the essential for us. Living from our knees is the secret of spiritual success. The kneeling David, right before his God, knew that his actions were being shaped by an Almighty God. It is a portrait of a small frame confidently running towards a "mountain" of a Goliath.

We face the ongoing crises in various regions of Africa. We acknowledge the realities of recruitment in the west. We continually face financial restraints. We dialogue about where and how to serve, The life of David has much to say to us. Only dependence upon the strong arm of the Lord can fortify us and make us effective in our ministry for the Lord.

I know that a kneeling David has much to say to Ruth and me, as we continue to learn to relate, to discover and prepare for transition into our new role as co-directors for the Sahara area of Africa. We count it a privilege today to kneel with you!

8

Reflections

*This letter, written to 100 Huntley Street as Bob and Ruth were preparing to appear on a program provides a summary of the deaths of their precious sons Ross and Timothy, and of their reaction to what happened.
It is a part of the legacy of faith they have left behind.*

There was a lot of excitement and anticipation in the letter which we wrote to family, friends and supporters in 1989 announcing our return to Canada for furlough. We had just completed four-and-a-half years with Wycliffe Bible Translators working as a pilot and teacher in Cameroon, West Africa.

Our children, Ross, Erin and Timothy were only six, four and one when we left for overseas. They had little memory of what they would be returning to in Canada. We can recall that during supper times we would talk about the differences they would find. We would tell them about the ice cream cones, the cartoons we would watch on TV, the visits we would make to Grandma's house, and even an odd trip to the place called McDonald's. We were already receiving letters telling us of the special summer trip our loved ones had planned for us and of the picnics we would enjoy. The thought of reunions of many kinds brought a unique joy to each member of our family.

Ross, now a boy of ten, was the one with deep feelings. He responded to those in need with emotion and spiritual sensitivity. He wanted to please others—even Mom and Dad. He loved to be active and energetic. At six years of age he joined in a 10 km race up and down the hills of Yaounde. He got into the cross-cultural scene and would even eat whatever was offered to him—including bush rat or fried grasshoppers.

Erin was now a girl of nine. Being the only girl she received all kinds of special attention. She was a great giggler and set us all off laughing until our sides would hurt. Erin could be a friendly flexible delight and sometimes so stubborn. She loved to dress up her little brother, as well as her African monkey whom we called "Georgie" like a girl.

Timothy was now a blond, brown-eyed shy boy of five. He kept silent until he was three as his siblings did all the needed talking for him. Tim had tremendous determination when he wanted to. One day he decided he was going to swim and did so for 20 laps of the pool. We remember the constant reading of Bible stories to him, while he curled up on our knee.

As a family of five we dragged our luggage onto the plane and worked our way back to Canada. It was en route that Erin began to feel sick and soon afterwards, Timothy. It was a Saturday night when we arrived in Toronto and were surrounded by our loving families as we came through the arrival doors. Needless to say we were tired but energized by the reunion. On Sunday evening Ross began to feel ill as well, so we decided to visit the family doctor the next morning. That Monday, following an explanation of where we had been and what we had been doing, the doctor examined the kids and decided that it was a case of strep throat and merely required antibiotics and rest. It was a slow beginning to our holiday, but we anticipated a quick recovery. By Wednesday, Erin was feeling much better, but not Ross and Tim. I called the doctor about this on Thursday evening and he suggested that it would not be worth seeing them right away but rather come to his office on Friday morning.

It was during the morning of June 23rd, that Ruth and I read the Daily Light after breakfast. I accidentally turned to April the 23rd—the title was "But the Lord was my support."

We were somewhat relieved that something substantial would be done as we drove to the doctor's office. We could never have imagined the events we were about to face that morning. The Daily Light reading had concluded with the verse, "*The Lord is my helper, I will not be afraid... it is God who arms me with strength.*"

The doctor who had diagnosed our children on Monday, first examined Ross and quickly dispatched us to the emergency ward of the hospital saying that it appeared he had hepatitis. We entered the doors of the hospital at 10:30 a.m. We were met by a Dr. Conners who had been with the Flying Doctors in Zambia, and might be able to identify anything tropical in nature. Earlier, we had suggested to our family doctor that it might be malaria. We helped as we could, speaking words of love and encouragement to our children as blood was drawn and IVs connected. Within a short time it was decided that Ruth should go with Timothy to McMaster Hospital and that I would stay with Ross and Erin at St. Joseph's.

Shortly after, Erin and I were separated from Ross and asked to wait in a side room. I remember a dear Roman Catholic sister with eyes of compassion, entering the room along with the doctor. They explained how serious our son's conditions were and Erin should be admitted as well. It was that afternoon, within two hours we heard the words, "We are sorry, but Timothy has died." And again, while surrounded by our family members, "Mr. and Mrs. Chapman, Ross is now gone." Malaria had not been diagnosed soon enough. I recall talking to God though eyes brimming with tears, "Yes my Father you are good, you are love, you know." Erin cried quietly as the reality of it entered her mind and heart. We all hugged her and tried to comfort her.

I drove with my parents to the hospital where Timothy's body lay. Ruth was coming back to be with Erin. I knew I had to see my little boy at rest, even if only for a moment. As I entered the draped off room, reached out and stroked his blond head and God spoke to me saying, "I am the resurrection and the life."

That night Ruth was admitted to hospital for hepatitis, and I was allowed to sleep in a cot alongside my wife and daughter. Our young nurse, a Christian, cared for us as best she knew how. Ruth and I held hands and sleep came.

I can still recall sitting in the back room of Grandma's where the boys had shared a pull-out bed and we had comforted them with sips of juice, a story, a cool washcloth. As I sat there I could see them in my minds eye. The tears began to sting my cheeks as I asked God why He hadn't told someone it was malaria. Why hadn't we reacted sooner? Why hadn't the doctor taken this more seriously?

Following the burial of the two small white coffins, one on top of the other, it took a real effort to enter back into daily life and routines. I remember dropping off Ruth at her sister's and heading to the bank. Driving alone in the car, I felt the frustration of my smallness and inability to change what had happened came over me. I was feeling robbed and cheated. I wanted my boys back. I wanted to hold them, to tell them how I loved them and tell them how much joy they brought into our lives. I wanted to play ball, go biking, run in the park. I hit the steering wheel as I drove. I parked the car and headed in, crying to God to help us with these kinds of adjustments. I lined up fearing that emotions would overtake me in public. A teller waved me over. She spoke kindly and didn't mind the fact that I didn't remember what forms had to be filled out and signed. It was just before I left that she leaned towards me and said, "I am so sorry about what has happened to your sons; I will be remembering you in my prayers." I thanked this sensitive stranger and quickly left. This time as I drove my heart was impressed by the fact that God had lovingly arranged that encounter just at a time when I needed a special reminder of His love and presence and control.

We freely communicated the temptations we felt throughout this tragedy. At one point I struggled with the "if only" syndrome. I recall one morning turning to Ruth and hugging her and saying, "This is a battle, it is a war, we need to be firm and take up the instruction in Ephesians to put on the whole armour of God." For many weeks the thoughts and emotions that first came to us upon waking required action on our part. Together, each morning, we quickly went to the

Word, and spent time listening to God instead of to our own imaginations.

Ruth and I believe that God graciously spared our daughter's life. She had the same exposure as the boys, and fell sick before them. We have thanked God that despite her age she showed an incredible resilience. Her childlike faith in where Ross and Timothy had gone was another witness of God's love. Often she would sense our pain and come to comfort us with her presence. Our common concern for her pulled us together in purposeful ways.

These are some of the emotions that I remember of the most significant testing that we have ever faced as husband and wife. A mutual friend of ours told us, not too long after our sons died, that more than 50% of marriages break up when a child dies. I believe that today we can testify to having a stronger and more solid relationship because of what God has allowed to enter into our marriage.

9

Heavenly Resources

"... weeping may remain for a night,
but rejoicing comes in the morning."

(Psalm 30:5)

To grapple with tragedy is not easy, even for those who believe implicity in the promises of the Lord. One naturally looks back on the events surrounding tragedy and sorrow, and wonders whether they could have been altered. Photos and memories indelibly reinforce the truth that though they are dead, they still speak to us because of their faith.

The faith chapter, Hebrews 11, includes the names of those who *"received God's approval because of their faith"* (verse 39), and the wonderful assurance that, *"God had far better things in mind for us that would also benefit them"* (verse 4, NLT). Faith, therefore, becomes transferable so that we are influenced by the lives of those who have left us.

The greatest temptation when the dearest ones we love have gone is to give up. Solitary sorrow seems to be the solution to our problems, and to escape to some island of isolation on which to mourn seems desirable. Often we drift on the sea of despair, without sight of anything that is permanently fixed. But then we are bolstered and helped by the keen sense of God's great grace. Hope and help come to us through various sources. As Paul reminds us, *"Hope does not disappoint us"* (Romans 5:5). The song by Howard Davies puts it into proper perspective:

> Many are the things I cannot understand,
>   All above me mystery I see;
> But the gift most wonderful from God's own hand
>   Surely is His gift of grace to me!
>
> Higher than the stars that reach eternity,
>   Broader than the boundaries of endless space,
> Is the boundless love of God that pardoned me;
>   O the wonder of His grace!

Life's trials can be endured because we know they are temporary. The resources of heaven belong to us as they come directly from the hand of the Lord. We survive because we belong to the Almighty and the truth of His sovereignty will never disappear. The assurance that our tomorrow with Him will transcend all else is the reason for renewed hope and joy. We are reminded "...rejoice that you participate in the sufferings of Christ, so that you may be overjoyed when His glory is revealed" (1 Peter 4:13). Although grief and suffering may try to destroy that joy, the paramount promise remains that Christ's joy can never be erased.

Providentially, the bodies of Bob and Ruth were found near the site of the air crash, and returned to Canada for burial the day before the memorial service in Hamilton. Their graves are within a few yards of their two sons, Ross and Timothy. For identification of Bob's earthly remains, the ring that Ruth had given him, years earlier, was the main source of information. Its inscription read "Ruth 1:16," not referring to his beloved wife, Ruth, but to the verse of Scripture that reads, "Where you go I will go." With certainty, we know where Bob has gone and that in heaven Ruth is with him. How prophetic was the engraving on the ring.

We continue to weep, for there is no shame in tears. Even Jesus wept at the grave of Lazarus. But the joy of the believer is not dependent or based upon external events, but on eternal verities. Joy comes as a supreme gift from the Holy Spirit. We look forward to that day when

> *He will remove all of their sorrows, and there will be no more death or sorrow or crying or pain. For the old world and its evils are gone forever* (Revelation 21:4 NLT).

Current testimonials from family members are an evidence of God's abiding grace and strength for each of us:

From daughter Erin:

"When asked to write about how I am doing and what I am doing, I was unsure of what to say. It is very difficult to describe what has gone on since my mom and dad died. Both life and death now have new meaning and feelings change daily, There are times when frustration, anger and even confusion are the only emotions that I feel. There are hopeful days when I recall some wonderful memories. Since the death of my parents, I have been so blessed by the prayers of so many people, as well as by the cards and the kind words spoken. These have really meant a lot to me. At times I really feel that is the reason I am able to keep going.

Following the memorial service in Hamilton, I went to Africa with my aunt and uncle, David and Carolyn. We visited the site of the accident in the Ivory Coast, and then went to Kenya. The most difficult thing was to go to my parent's apartment in Nairobi. To see the place exactly as they had left it and to dispose of their personal possessions was heartbreaking. After a few days, I went to Cameroon, back to where I had spent most of my childhood and teen years. I stayed with the Golding family who have four daughters, two of whom are about my age. It was a real blessing to be with them and we had some wonderful times together. Friends were visiting from other countries, so it was good to be with them as well. There was time to visit a number of places, and also to spend time with people who had known my parents.

After returning to Canada, I visited with family and friends and then returned to Trinity Western University for my studies. I have just completed my first semester of my junior year in international studies. This summer, I will be taking a further course at Trinity, and spending time with family and friends. I am so thankful that I have the resources to make this possible. Although it has been several months since the accident, I still miss my parents like it was yesterday. Every day there are so many things that remind me of them. I miss their advice and counsel on issues that I face, especially at a time in life when there are so many decisions to be made. It is not easy to trust in God, but I know that is really all I can do as I face the unknown future."

From Sylvia, Ruth's sister:

"It is still hard to believe that Ruth and Bob have gone. Although it has been some months since the accident, often I think, 'I must remember to tell Ruth and Bob about that.' Or, 'when Bob and Ruth come home, it would be great to do this or that together.' Of course, they have gone 'Home' and we cannot do anything together again in this life. The struggle and questioning of 'why the plane crashed and why they weren't among the survivors' has eased. But times of questioning and profound sadness still come.

"A short time after their death, my mother's eyesight deteriorated so much that she was declared legally blind. Almost a year to the day, she moved from her home of 53 years to an apartment close to our home. At 86, Mom Harding continues to enjoy the women's home league, Bible study, the golden agers and Sunday worship. She is a great blessing from God. On May 5, 2001 her first grandchild, our son Scott, was married.

"We are grateful for the incredible number of expressions of sympathy received after Bob and Ruth's death. We continue to meet people who speak of the wonderful example they have left. I believe that the purpose of this book is to influence others for the Lord, and to challenge them for Christian service. We remember the many fun times we shared specially when all ten of us lived under the same roof for a year, when Bob was travelling to Toronto to study aircraft maintenance. We are constantly inspired by their selfless love for God and their boundless love for each other. Everything they did in life pointed us to

Jesus their Redeemer, Jesus God's own Son
Blessed Lamb of God, Messiah, Holy One.

"When I sing verse three, my eyes are filled with tears:

When I stand in Glory, I will see His face,
And there I'll serve my King forever, in that holy place..."

Carolyn, Bob's sister, wrote:

"Several months have passed since the airplane crash took the lives of Bob and Ruth. It has been a difficult time, filled with questions, tears, guilt and even denial. I find it difficult to realize that they are no longer in this world. Part of me wants to hold on to the expectation of postcards, e-mails and visits. I catch myself making plans for our next encounter and thinking of things I would like to tell them. Then the stark reality of the crash sinks in and the tears well up inside of me. Bob and Ruth were often gone for months or even years, and the separation from them was never easy.

"My personal experiences have made me realize that we as Christians are not promised tomorrow, or are we immune from tragedy or heartache. As the song says, 'The days I cannot see have all been planned for me, His way is best you see, I'm in His hands.' I often ask myself, 'Could this have been part of God's plan?' We will not know in this life, but we can be assured and comforted that God's plan is best. We can thank God for the beautiful memories we hold in our hearts and of the genuine interest that Bob and Ruth took in everyone they met. They truly practiced lifestyle evangelism, and enjoyed life fully.

"When the realization of their deaths hit me, I thought of something that Erin said to her parents on the death of her brothers: 'Why be so sad when you think of them? They are in a much better and happier place than we are.' I hold on to that thought when I am feeling sad and sorry for myself, and remember that one day we will be together again and what a day of rejoicing that will be."

A dear friend, Ruby Ward operated Lockyer's Florist shop in Picton, Ontario. When her mother died, Ruby decided to retain the home as a place of rest and refreshment for Salvation Army officers and Christian friends, at no charge. She would stock the refrigerator with food and place flowers in many of the rooms. Shortly after the deaths of our grandsons, we along with Bob and Ruth spent several days in this home. Together we shared our sorrows, tears and memories. Recently, while leafing through my NKJV version of the New Testament and Psalms, I found a verse I had marked on July 5th, 1989. It reads, "...*put my tears into Your bottle; Are they not in Your book?*" (Psalm 56:8). Once more, God came with special revelation and uplift in remembrance of this wonderful truth. How good to know that He does store our tears in His memory book.

In my bedroom, in the Chapman home in London, Ontario when I was a boy, was a motto on the wall that read, "Only one life will soon be past, Only what's done for Christ will last" followed by this text, "For to me to live is Christ." This is a fitting epitaph to our loved ones.

In a very practical way, to preserve the legacy left by Bob and Ruth, Wycliffe Bible Translators are building a 11,700 square foot facility in Yaounde, Cameroon costing $545,000. This will be named the CABTAL Chapman Centre. It will house the offices, training rooms and accommodation services needed to advance into the languages of Cameroon that still need God's Word. News has been received that the sod turning for this memorial building took place on the 31st of

July, 2001, with an expected opening in the year 2003. To help fulfill this vision, several thousand dollars have been contributed in memorial gifts by relatives and friends along with CABTAL members and donors in Cameroon, as well as the Canada and Bermuda Territory of The Salvation Army.

TO GOD BE ALL THE GLORY!

Saviour, in this hour of sorrow
Thou art solace, Thou art near.
Dark this night, but oh! tomorrow
Joy will triumph over tears.
What if grief engulf the valley?
There is glory on the hill!
Faith can see, and hope will rally
Hearts that trust the Father's will.

O'er the eastern skyline, breaking
Faint but lustrous rays of grace,
Portent of the new day, making
Promise of Thine unveiled face.
Shining, ere the Sun arises
Cheering, guiding, til the dawn
Gladdens us with God's surprises
When the night at last is come.

O Thou rising star of morning,
Lovely is Thy holy light,
Beautiful is Thine adorning
Thou art all my soul's delight.
In that day that lasts forever
We shall see Thee as Thou art.
We shall know Thee, Lord, and never
From Thy dwelling-place depart.

—Commissioner Edward J. Read
October 1, 1927–August 9, 2000
Sent on February 6, 2000